Microsoft Azure Administrator

Study Guide & Exam Prep

A catalogue record for this book is available from the British Library.

ISBN: 978-1-911064-08-4

Published by Black Chili Limited

For more information, please email publications@blackchili.co.uk

Masculine pronouns such as 'He' and 'His' are used throughout this publication for consistency, but no gender bias is intended.

Microsoft Azure Administrator:
AZ-104 –Study Guide & Exam Prep

INTRODUCTION 1

ABOUT THE AUTHOR 5

ACCOUNTS AND SUBSCRIPTIONS 7

ACCOUNT HIERARCHY 7
DOMAIN SERVICES 7
AZURE AD 8
AZURE AD PRICING 8

RESOURCE GROUPS AND TAGGING 9

RBAC 9

STORAGE 11

AZURE SQL SERVICES 11
AZURE STORAGE 12
STORAGE ACCOUNTS 13
MANAGE PERMISSIONS 16
ENCRYPTION KEYS & KEY VAULT 16
CUSTOM DOMAINS 17
IMPORT/EXPORT 17

VIRTUAL MACHINES 19

SUPPORTED OSES: 20
WINDOWS 20
LINUX 21
VM LIMITATIONS 21
POWERSHELL DSC 21
CUSTOM SCRIPT EXTENSIONS 22
VM AVAILABILITY 22
AVAILABILITY ZONES 23

VM Scaling 23
VM Storage Overview 23
Disk Caching 25
Disk Encryption 26

ARM TEMPLATES 27

Containers 28

APP SERVICES 29

App Service Monitoring 30
Azure Web App Diagnostic Logs: 31
App Server Settings 32
Deployment slots 33

NETWORKING 35

Internet Access and DNS 35
Network Security 36
Network Security Groups 37
Key networking limits 38
Azure Firewall 38
Azure Load Balancer 39
Hybrid connectivity options 40
VPN Gateway SKUs 41
Routing and Peering 43
Azure Monitoring 44

BACKUP 47

Azure Site Recovery (ASR) 48
Recovery Options 49

CONTACTING THE AUTHOR 51

Introduction

Cloud computing has completely transformed the technology landscape, in what seems like a heartbeat. This guide is designed for readers with a level of familiarity with both IT infrastructure concepts and Microsoft Azure. It assumes you are preparing for an associate level exam on Microsoft Azure components, and is not intended to provide an introduction to the fundamentals of Microsoft Azure.

The contents of this book were built by the author from his journey in passing the related exam.

Cloud Computing is the delivery of computing services such as servers, storage, databases, networking, software, analytics, intelligence, and more, over the Cloud (Internet).

Cloud Computing provides an alternative to the traditional datacentre. If you own or operate a datacentre, everything needs to be managed – the premises, power, cooling, purchasing and installing hardware, virtualisation, installing the operating system, and any applications, setting up the networking, routing and network security, and data storage. You are then responsible for the full lifecycle – all the maintenance and eventual decommissioning.

But if we choose Cloud Computing, a third-party cloud vendor is responsible for datacentre operations. They also provide a wide variety of servers, software, storage and platform as a service options. We consume whatever services we wish and are typically charged based on usage.

There are three main flavours of Cloud Computing – Public, Private, and Hybrid.

Public Cloud services are owned and operated by a third-party cloud service provider. They deliver computing resources such as servers, software, and storage. Providing a virtual datacentre over the internet. Microsoft Azure would be an example of a Public Cloud service.

Private Cloud services are those built to be exclusively used inside a single business or organisation. A private cloud may be physically located in company-operated premises or hosted by a third-party. Private Clouds typically consist of server and storage infrastructure, upon which many servers and services are virtualised. This is typically a much more costly option.

Hybrid cloud is a combination of public and private clouds, bridged together by technology that allows data and applications to be shared between them. Hybrid cloud provides flexibility and more deployment options to the business.

Cloud services are typically badged 'as a Service', and you'll see 'aaS' a good deal. Examples of high-level service types are:

Infrastructure as a Service (IaaS): Think of IaaS as the rental of traditional infrastructure elements like servers, storage, networks, operating systems and such from a cloud service vendor. We can create virtual machines running Windows or Linux and install anything we need on them as required. Using IaaS gives the customer freedom from hardware maintenance and hypervisor management, but everything beyond that is managed by the customer. The customer is in total control of systems running on managed infrastructure. Azure VMs would be an example of IaaS.

Platform as a Service (PaaS): The PaaS family of services provide on-demand environments for developing, testing, delivering, and managing software applications. The customer is responsible for applications and services, and the PaaS vendor provides the ability to deploy and run them. PaaS lacks the total customer control of IaaS, but has the advantage of reducing customer responsibility to the application tier, with everything else managed by the cloud services vendor. Azure SQL would be an example of a PaaS service.

Software as a Service (SaaS): SaaS covers the centrally hosted and managed software services provided direct to end-users. SaaS delivers software over the internet, on-demand, and typically on a subscription basis. Microsoft One Drive, Dropbox, WordPress, Office 365, and Amazon Kindle. SaaS is used to minimize the operational cost to the maximum extent.

In the following pages you will find everything the author collated in his study of AZ-104: Microsoft Azure Administration, to become a Certified Azure Administrator. This is an associate level qualification, and a solid familiarity with Microsoft Azure is expected. Appreciation of common IT infrastructure concepts is expected.

The AZ-104 examination has no pre-requisites, but if you find the material in this book too advanced, consider completing Microsoft Azure Fundamentals first as an introduction.

About the Author

I left University with an English Literature degree and like most people with English degrees who have no inclination to go into teaching; I had no idea what I was going to do. I fell into a resourcing job for a recruitment company... calling people and talking to them on the phone about technology jobs I didn't understand, and getting paid minimum wage. I have that terrible job to thank for setting my future direction.

My last day at that company started uneventfully enough, until one of the many people I called that day unwittingly showed me the light. He was pretty horrible actually – I'd called him regarding a contract that was obviously some way beneath him. He was direct, to put it mildly – and his parting words were, 'So you can update your records, I wouldn't take a permanent role for less than £250K'. **Two hundred and fifty *thousand* pounds?** (and this was in 1999!) At the rate I was going that would be 25 years' wages. And that was my light bulb moment.

I looked at the skills required for some of the serious consultancy roles, I was spending my days trying to fill, then researched what the jobs that fed those sorts of positions were. Having followed my nose to the entry level of the field, I set about acquiring the skills required to get through the door. I worked my way through the ranks in several jobs, which at the time I didn't much appreciate, all of which allowed me to build solid experience with some of the biggest companies in the world.

I studied for professional qualifications on my own time, self-funding courses and exams – investing in myself. I have been Microsoft Certified since 1999, on Windows NT4!

My Microsoft Certifications include:

Microsoft Certified Azure Architect Expert
Microsoft Certified Azure Security Engineer
Microsoft Certified Azure Administrator
Microsoft Certified Systems Engineer
Microsoft Certified Administrator
Microsoft Certified Professional

I also hold certifications from Amazon, Novell, Forcepoint and TOGAF, amongst others.

Certifications have helped me secure ever-more senior positions in large companies and have seen my annual salary increase many times over since I started on the certification trail in 1999. All my cloud certifications have been gained without classroom teaching, using Microsoft Learn content, and other material freely available on the Internet. Access to, and familiarity with, the Azure Portal and CLI will be a massive advantage as you approach the exam.

You will find my professional profile on LinkedIn here:

https://www.linkedin.com/in/renhimself/

Accounts and Subscriptions

Account Hierarchy

An Enterprise account (http://ea.azure.com) brings with it the enterprise, and departments within, which then contain accounts that are equivalently the root of a standard Azure account. Accounts include subscriptions, holding resource groups and resources. Management Groups can be used to apply similar settings to multiple subscriptions for ease of administration.

One Enterprise can have many departments. One department can hold many accounts, and one account can hold many subscriptions.

Domain Services

Azure Active Directory (AAD) - AD for Cloud, usually the same as your O365 directory service. Can sync with on-prem AD.

Active Directory Domain Services (ADDS) is a legacy AD since Windows 2000, which uses traditional Kerberos and LDAP functionality. Deployed on Windows OS, usually on VMs.

Azure Active Directory Domain Services (AADDS) provides managed domain services. Allows you to consume domain services without having to maintain domain controllers etc. This allows domain join, group policy, LDAP, Kerberos, NTLM.

Azure AD

Enterprise Identity Solution with single sign-on. MFA for security and self-service password resets as well as request access to specific apps and services.

Security groups and O365 groups. Assign users to groups, assign groups to roles for access to resources.

P2 premium required for self-service password reset functionality. Can be allowed for nobody, specific users, or all users. Users can be authenticated for password resets via mobile app code, Email, Mobile phone, Office phone or security questions.

Azure AD Pricing

Free version has a 500,000-object limit. No limit on the others. Free & Basic has a 10 app SSO limit per user.

Free does not allow group-based access management, self-service password reset, company branding on login pages, application proxy.

Most useful features are premium, with P2 adding identity protection, privileged identity management, 3rd party MFA integration, Access reviews, SharePoint Limited access, and CAS proxy.

Resource Groups and Tagging

Tags can be applied to subscriptions, resource groups or individual resources. Resource level makes sense. You can have up to 15 tags to help identify location, purpose, cost centre, business unit etc. Makes admin easier.

RBAC

Role Based Access Control

Create users' apps and groups, then assign those entities to objects in Azure via specific roles. Built in Azure roles - Owner - full access to everything, including giving other people access. Contributor can do everything an owner can do, except for granting access to others. Reader as it says - can view existing resources but cannot create anything. There are also many application specific roles for tasks such as API management, app insights, automation, backup etc. Roles can be assigned to users, groups, applications and VMs.

Roles include actions, which define what holders of that role can do - actions define what you can with not actions stating what you cannot. Write enables the role holder to put, post, patch, delete and any 'modify' type action. Read covers GET actions.

Get-AzureRMRoleDefinitions - to get latest roles

RBAC custom roles also available, each tenant can have up to 2000 roles. Use any combination of Actions and NotActions to shape a role as required. These can also be assigned to Subscriptions, Resource Groups or Resources as required.

Storage

Types of Data - Structured, semi structured, and unstructured. Structured data adheres to a schema, all the data has the same field or properties - may be stored in database tables in rows and columns, and relies on keys to indicate how one row in a table relates to data in another row of another table. Also known as relational data.

Semi structured data uses tags and keys to organise and provide a hierarchy for the data. Often referred to as NoSQL or non-relational data. Unstructured data has no designated structure or restrictions on data type - could be blob storage for example, holding PDFs, Office docs, images, scripts, movie files etc. Enterprises struggle to manage and tap into insights from their unstructured data.

Azure SQL Services

Azure is a relational database as a PaaS service - latest version of SQL where you can create new or migrate existing databases using the Microsoft Data Migration Assistant. Key features are predictable performance measured in database throughput units (DTUs), High Compatibility - supporting existing SQL client applications via tubular database stream (TDS) endpoint, and simplified management via SQL server-specific Azure tools. MS manage the platform.

3 database tiers - basic is for single user small databases, usually dev/test and 5DTU capable. Standard is for medium sized databases that require multiple concurrent connections. Good for cloud apps, workgroups, and web apps. 10-100 DTUs. Premium is for large databases that must support a large number of concurrent connections and operations, used for mission-critical apps 100-800 DTUs.

Azure SQL Managed Instances - higher compatibility with legacy workloads.

Third party databases in Azure - Managed. MySQL and PostgreSQL - built in HA at no additional cost, predictable performance, pay as you go, auto-scaling, encryption at rest and in transit, automatic backup with point in time restore up to 35 days and enterprise grade security and compliance.

Third party databases in Azure - Non-Managed. Windows Azure VMs hosting MySQL, Linux VMs hosting MySQL, ClearDB offering managed MySQL instance.

Azure Storage

Blob Storage - unstructured storage for images, video, files of any type. Use cases include streaming video and images direct to users, backup or DR of data, and archiving.

Azure File Services - SMB file shares and permissions. Supports SMB 2.1 (unsecured) and

3.0 (secured) - shares can be mounted on Windows, Linux, or Mac. Azure file sync can be used to sync file servers on-prem with Azure Files.

Table Storage - NoSQL key-value store with schema less design. Can hold structured or unstructured data and can be accessed using the OData protocol and LINQ queries WCF data service .NET libraries.

Queue Storage - can be used to store and deliver messages for applications. A single queue message can be up to 64KB in size, and a queue can contain millions of messages, up to the total capacity limit of the storage account.

Storage Accounts

Blob storage overview - storage account - container - data objects. 3 account types - General Purpose v1 (GPv1), Blob Account and General Purpose v2 (GPv2) - GPv2 being the most used option. GPb2 allows the creation of page blobs, block blobs, the storage of VM disks - basically GPv2 permits storage of pretty much anything.

A block blob is ideal for storing text or binary files, a single block blob can hold up to 50,000 blocks of up to 100MB each for a total capacity of 4.75TB - use case is application data storage. Append blobs are optimised for append operations, such as logging. A Page

Blob is more efficient for read-write operations, used by Azure VMs with a maximum size of 8TB.

Storage tiers come with GPv2 - hot storage has the highest storage cost but lowest access cost - a good choice for frequently used data. Cold storage has lower storage costs but higher access cost, so better for infrequently used data (designed for data that will be used less frequently than every 30 days).

It is possible to move between tiers, but penalty fees are incurred. Archive storage has the lowest storage cost but the highest retrieval cost. When a blob is in archive storage it is offline and cannot be read - it must be pulled back to storage where it can be read to be accessed, so there is a time delay. Auto-tiering automation can be used to move data across tiers according to pre-set criteria.

Replication options for storage accounts from locally redundant storage (LRS) through zone and geo-redundant. There are also specific read-access replication tiers available.

LRS - default, and available for all storage account types. Data is replicated 3 times within a datacentre. Synchronous replication ensures all copies are up to date. 99.9% availability SLA (DR), but 11 9s durability (loss or corruption). ZRS is only available on GPv2 and is the multi-AZ version of LRS - still within a region, but in multiple DCs. Durability of data on ZRS increases to 12 9s. GRS is like LRS but makes a further 3 copies to an adjacent region asynchronously so there is a slight delay. The secondary GRS location is not available unless the primary goes offline. RA-GRS is the read access version of GRS, allowing the secondary location to be readable. RA-GRS raises the read operation SLA to 99.99% availability, with write operations remaining at 99.9% due to the single region still being in control of write and update operations. Microsoft control the failover of GRS and RA-GRS

Network access - Public (Default), Public Endpoint (selected networks that you choose can access) or Private Endpoint (uses a private IP and all traffic over the MS network). Containers within the storage account have their own network access settings, independent of the storage account.

Blob soft delete permits the recovery of deleted files up to a retention period you specify.

Virtual disks are used for when there is no need to access data outside of the associated VM.

Download and use storage explorer to manipulate blob storage accounts and their content, move files etc. AZ Copy is a command line utility used for copying data to and from a storage account.

Microsoft require that you be granted the storage blob data contributor role against a storage account, regardless of the other roles you hold when copying files into blob storage.

A SAS token is required to copy data from a storage account using AZ Copy. AZ Copy by default uploads data into block blobs. To upload files as Append Blobs or Page Blobs use the flag --blob-type=[PageBlob | AppendBlob].

Manage Permissions

Container access policies. Default is private, so nobody else can access. Blob permission allows anonymous read access for blobs only. Container allows anonymous read access for containers and blobs.

SAS Shared Access Signatures are appended to access URLS to control who, what where and when can access storage locations referenced. Account SAS tokens are granted at the account level. Service SAS tokens are used to grant access to specific services within a storage account. All SAS tokens are encrypted using hash-based message authentication.

Encryption Keys & Key Vault

User creates a storage account and enables Storage Service Encryption (SSE), user writes data into blob. Azure storage is accessed using the key, which can optionally be wrapped and unwrapped using an HSM. Customer managed keys also available.

Custom Domains

Custom domains can be used for Storage, Blob and Root containers. This can be done via your domain DNS directly using a CNAME. This method is quicker but results in downtime as Azure must verify the domain registration. Or you use the 'asverify' subdomain. set up verify.yourdomain.com to:

asverify.yourstorageaccount.blob.core.indows.net

Once this step complete you can create a CNAME record in DNS that points to youraccount.blob.core.windows.net. Using this method does not result in downtime and to use this method, select 'use indirect CNAME validation' checkbox during setup.

Import/Export

Data Migration to cloud, content distribution, backup and data recovery are all use cases. The import/export service can be accessed via the Azure portal and used to trach import and export jobs. There is also a command line tool which can prepare disks that are shipped, copying data to drives, encrypting data with bit locker, generating drive journal files, determining number of drives. Use V1 for blob and V2 for files.

Disks for Import Export can be HDD or SSD. Import Jobs you ship drives to MS for Import in to Azure. For export jobs you ship empty drives for the export(s).

Azure File Sync can be used to sync a share on an on-prem server with Azure. Create a storage account. Create a files container, create a group and a storage endpoint. Set up the server and create a server endpoint before setting up the sync.

Virtual Machines

Hardware tier abstracted, addition of hypervisor and ability to run multiple OSes on a single physical system. In Azure, MS manage the hardware and hypervisor.

A - the first type MS introduced. General purpose, with 'Basic' being for dev/test/

B - Burstable, ability to go 100% on CPU when required. Conserves credits in periods of low use for execution when utilisation increases.

D - General purpose built for enterprise apps, DS instances offer premium storage

E - Memory optimised with high memory to CPU ratio, ES has premium storage

F - CPU optimised. FS offers premium storage

G - Godzilla - Very large instances for large databases and big data use case.

H - High performance compute. For very high-end computational needs such as molecular modelling and scientific applications.

L - Storage optimised - higher disk throughput and I/O

M - Large memory. Allows up to 3.5TB of RAM

N - GPU enabled

SAP HANA on Azure Certified Instances - specialised instances built and certified for SAP HANA.

Specialisations - **S** for premium storage, **M** for larger memory, **R** for remote direct memory access (RDMA)

Azure Compute Units - A series is the benchmark at 100 ACU, all others use that as a comparison.

Supported OSes:

Windows

Windows 2003 and alter are supported or deployment but must bring own image and there is no marketplace support and no MS support whatsoever. Must have your own customer support agreement.

Windows Server 2008 R2 is supported, with a specific support matrix for server roles - not all are supported.

Windows Server 2012 is supported, with datacenter version available in the marketplace.

Windows Server 2016 is supported, with datacenter and nano versions available in the marketplace.

Windows 10 Pro and Enterprise are available in the marketplace

Linux

- CentOS 6.3+, 7.0+
- CoreOS 40140+
- Debian 7.9+, 8.2+
- Oracle Linux 6.4+, 7.0+
- Red Hat Enterprise Linux RHEL 6.7+, 7.1+
- SUSE Linux SLES / SLES for SAP 11 SP4. 12 SP1+
- openSUSE Leap 42.2+

VM Limitations

Regional limitations on Azure services. A and B instance types particularly are available in a reduced number of regions. Good to take note of region pairs a well and distribute VMs such as to avoid total outage during patching or issue.

Some VM usernames are also restricted - administrator, admin, user, user1, test, user2, test1, user3, admin1, 1, 123, a, actuser, admin, admin2, aspnet, backup, console, david, guest, john, owner, root, server, sql, support, support_388945a0, sys, test2, test3, user4 & user5 cannot be used.

PowerShell DSC

Azure provides configuration management extensions for puppet, Chef and PowerShell. PowerShell DSC lacks the enterprise-level configuration management options for multiple nodes and cloud / on-prem of puppet and chef.

PowerShell DCS components: Configurations - scripts. Resources - the code keeping configuration in a specified state. Logical Configuration Manager is the engine that connects the other two.

Custom Script Extensions

Execute VM tasks without logging in to the VM. Upload via portal or download scripts from Azure Blob storage or GitHub. Can also be automated with PowerShell. No need for login credentials required for the VM, the VM also does not need an accessible IP and custom extensions are easy to implement. However, the custom extension must be enabled on each VM you want to run it, and the VMs will need Internet access if using GitHub or Blob storage for scripts. It is also slow.

VM Availability

Potential for VM impact - planned maintenance, unplanned hardware maintenance or unexpected downtime. Availability sets are groups of two or more machines that are separated based on fault domains and update domains. A fault domain is a rack with its own power and networking. There are typically 3 fault domains in an availability set. Within the availability set there will also be update domains, which are collections of physical host machines updated together, but only one group will updated at a time. Each application tier needs to be spread across a fault domain and across update domains.

Availability Zones

Not available in every region. 99.99% availability. Work like Availability sets and are succeeding availability sets - so where zones are available, sets ae not. Separate DCs in the same region. No performance impact but much improved resilience.

VM Scaling

Scale sets allow horizontal scaling to meet demand. Virtual Machine Scale Sets (VMSS). You configured the scale set - how many macnines and their size. You can elect to auto-scale or manage it manually. Set minimum and maximum machine counts and scale out based on metrics in infrastructure or applications. Can also scale out on a schedule. Remember to account for active sessions when you scale in by using Redis cache etc.

VM Storage Overview

Standard HDD storage - cheapest option but IOPSS are also the lowest.

Standard SSD - recommended for most workloads, max throughput 500MB/S per disk and Max IOPS 2000 per disk

Premium Storage - SDD, highest performance and lowest latency. 750MB/S throughput and 7500 max IOPS per disk.

Managed disk standard storage sizes - S4 - 32GB, S6 - 64, S10 - 128 - S20 - 512, S30 - 1024, S40 - 2048, S50 – 4095

Standard SSD Storage disk sizings are the same as above, but E instead of S. Max IOPS is 120 on E4, 240 on E6 and 500 on all sizes beyond. Throughput is 25MB/S on E4, 50MB/S on E6 and 60MB/S beyond.

Premium SSD sizes as before, but with 'P' identifier. Max available IOPS are 120,240,500,1100,2300,500,7500,7500.

Throughput 25MB/s, 50MB/s, 100MB/s, 125MB/s, 150MB/s, 200MB/s, 250MB/s, 250MB/s.

Ultra SSD in preview with massive IOPS and throughput

VM Limits - make sure your VM can handle the disk IOPS you have paid for, otherwise your high-performance disk will be constrained by the VM.

Managed or Unmanaged? Unmanaged are DIY with a management overhead, and 20000 IOPS per storage account limit, but they are supported by all replication modes. Managed disks are the simplest option as they are MS managed, but they also only support LRS replication.

LRS - locally replicated, 3 copies within an availability zone.

ZRS - replicated across zones within a region - 3 copies across one or two datacenters.

GRS - replicated to a second region - so basically ZRS x 2 regions.

RA-GRS - as before, but the data is available for read only in the second region. It is not accessible in GRS.

Disk Caching

Method to improve performance of VHDs, utilising RAM and SSD drives on the underlying VM Host. Available on standard and premium disks - OS disks default to read/write caching but can be changed to read-only. Data disks default to non but can be read-only or read/write caching enabled. Read-only can improve latency and provide higher IOPS, read/write you need to ensure you have a method to write data from the cache to persistent disks to avoid data loss.

Disk Encryption

Bit locker for Windows, DM-Crypt for Linux. Integrates with Key Vault for encryption key management. Most scenarios support encryption, but you cannot encrypt basic tier VM disks. You cannot disable encryption on the OS or data drive of a Linux VM when the OS disk is encrypted.

You cannot encrypt OS Drive for Linux VMs in a scale set. Encryption on top of software RAID does not work, encrypting custom images on Linux VMs and integration with on-prem keys does not work (must use key vault). Azure files, NFS, dynamic volumes and ephemeral OS disks are also not encryption candidates.

Encryption pre-requisites - minimum 2GB RAM for Windows or Linux VMs, 8GB minimum required to encrypt OS and data on Linux (2* data disk volume). Windows 8 and later, Windows Server 2008 R2 and later and Linux. Networking - connectivity to AAD, key vault and Azure storage required. Key Vault must be enabled for encryption, deployment, and template deployment (if required).

Encryption config options - PowerShell, Azure CLI or ARM Templates.

ARM Templates

Resources get put in resource groups, the resource provider is the provider that controls the interactions with resource groups, enabling the deployment of templated resources to a resource group.

ARM templates are infrastructure as code. A JSON file that states how a resource should be deployed. UI deployed resources display the code used to deploy them, which can be copied out and edited, or used as a template if required. Quick start templates are also available via the Microsoft site and GitHub - ARM templates for loads of systems and services.

File types - The AR template itself describes the configuration of your infrastructure via a JSON file. An optional ARM template parameter file can be introduced to separate your parameters. Deployment scripts and PowerShell scripts used to apply the template to Azure.

Template constructs - Parameters define the inputs to pass in to ARM templates during deployment, Variables can be used to simplify the template, Resources are the Azure objects to create or update, Outputs allow you to specify the values returned after the ARM deployment is complete.

ARM Templates and linking templates - templates can be linked to other templates in two ways - 1) Inline, where the entire template is included in the body of another template, or 2) External, with an inline or external parameter set.

3 Key ARM template functions for the exam - Copy, which allows a resource to be created and duplicated. copyIndex(), which allows for the creation of unique resources by concatenating with a value pulled in from elsewhere, and dependsOn which as the name suggests defines other objects that must exist for the object about to be created.

You can generate an automation script from a resource group or resource by clicking the link in the menu. You will be shown JSON content sufficient to recreate the object selected.

Containers

A docker container is a standardised package for software and dependencies, a way to isolate apps from each other which works with Linux and Windows and allows separate apps to share the same OS kernel. Breaking an app into separate microservices makes it easier to manage - making each component independently scalable, stateless, highly available by design. Horizontal scaling rather than traditional vertical.

App Services

Azure App Services consist of the following:

Web Apps, Mobile Apps, Logic Apps and API Apps. Web apps were formerly known as websites - auto-scaling, highly available and include DevOps features. Mobile Apps allow the build of a mobile device backend to build native apps for iOS, Android, Windows, and cross-core platform apps.

Logic Apps automate business processes, creating orchestration workflows. Every time your app calls an API do some task / ingest data from a storage blob or external SaaS service / check tweets or #SLACK messages from a specific account - and then do 'stuff'. API apps allow the easy creation, consumption and calling of APIs, with options to use APIs you create or external API services.

Security features - Apps run on isolated VMs and are ISO, SOC and PCI compliant. Fully AAD integrated with managed service identities. Custom domains are supported, as is SSL/TLS including custom certificates using wildcards or subject alternate names. Supports multiple authentication protocols - OAuth, OpenID, and Microsoft AAD. Also integrates with WAF. DevOps features include CI/CD, IDE Tool Integration and Deployment slots.

App Service Plans - configure the subscription the plan belongs to, the location, the pricing tier and instance size. Then set up scale counts, scaling rules and scale up to increase resources associated with the app service plan.

App service plan pricing tiers - free and shared operate on shared compute resources, multiple apps including those of other customers. CPU quotas are allocated to each app that runs - resources cannot be scaled out. For scaling out, you would need to use the dedicated compute resources of the basic, standard, premium and isolated tiers.

App service plan guidance - create a plan for a specific application, deploy app services to support the application, do not use a single plan for every web app, combine app services vs. Mass VM creation, combine other services in the same resource group.

App Service Environments (ASE) - Fully isolated environments for high performing apps requiring high CPU or memory. Any shared platform can suffer from contention. 2 ways to deploy - Internal or External depending on whether you want public or private presentation. Created in a subnet of a VNet, which achieves isolation. ASEs may take some time to start up, as compute is commissioned.

App Service Monitoring

Management Tools - Management portal, Kudu, Visual Studio, PowerShell & CLI. Service plan metrics include CPU, Memory, Data In/

Out (bandwidth), Disk queue length and http queue length.

Free and shared app quotas - CPU (Short) - amount of CPU allowed for this application in a 5-minute interval. CPU (Day) Total CPU allowed in a day, resets at midnight. Memory - total allowed for an application, Bandwidth - resets every day. Filesystem - total storage allowed. Exceeding the quota on CPU or bandwidth results in the app stopping until the quota resets. Exceeding memory quota results in an app restart, and exceeding the filesystem quota means all write operations, including logging, will fail.

Azure Web App Diagnostic Logs:

- Application - Error, Warning, Information and Verbose logging levels
- Web Server - web server logging, detailed error message and failed request tracing

Application logs are stored in Application/, failed request traces in W3SVC##########/, Detailed errors in DetailedErrors/, Web Server Logs in http/RawLogs and deployment logs in /Git.

App Insights - metric alerts tell you when a threshold is crossed. Web Tests tell you when a site is unavailable or responding slowly. Proactive diagnostics are triggered when something out of the ordinary occurs - these are automatically configured based on historical performance and activity patterns.

App Server Settings

.NET is on by default v4.7, can also be v3.5
PHP is on by default v5.5, can also be off, v5.6, v5.7, v7.0 or v7.1
Java is off by default, but 7.8 is supported
Python is off by default, can be v2.7 or v3.4
Platform determines x32 or x64, with x64 requiring basic or standard mode.
Web Sockets is off by default, can be on.
Always on is off by default, can be on
Auto-swap automatically moves slot into production when code is pushed into it. On by default.

Connection strings allow us to set database config per slot. It is a variable instead of a config file, and secure as it does not store as a file. - SQL.CONNSTR for example. Custom also available.

Handler mappings have an extension for the file to be handler, a processor path which is the path to the script processor and optional additional arguments which can be used to add extra commands for the script processor.

Virtual applications and directories - a virtual directory that users take to access the application. A physical path to the directory or application and the application - a virtual directory by default that must be selected by default for a web app.

To use a custom domain simply register a domain, adda suitable DNS record and associate with the web app.

Deployment slots

Allow the deployment of an app to non-production slots to stage them prior to Live. Applies to Web Apps on Windows and Linux, and Mobile Apps. It reduces risk and increases speed. A staging slot can be swapped to production seamlessly, as well as back to staging again if required.

Most settings are swapped from staging to production -general settings such as framework version, x32, web sockets etc. App settings (though they can be set per slot), connection strings (can be set per slot), handler mappings, Monitoring, and diagnostic settings, webjobs content. However, publishing endpoints, custom domain names, SSL certs and bindings, scale settings and webjob schedulers are not swapped.

Networking

Basic concept of on-prem systems and services connecting either via an encrypted tunnel over the Internet, or via direct connection to a Virtual network in Azure which may hold various subnets, systems, and services. Access to those systems can be filtered as required.

VNets contain subnets (must have at least 1 subnet), and by default subnets within a VNet can route to each other. NSGs can be used to filter traffic between them. VNets are isolated from each other unless we decide otherwise. Internet access is enabled by default. We can connect multiple Azure resources such as web apps and services, with all systems, apps and services sharing a VNet boundary if we so desire.

VNets can be connected together, as well as being connected to on-prem. VNets are the primary building block for Azure networking, they are a private network in Azure based on your address space prefix. You can create subnets in your VNets with you IP ranges. You can bring your own DNS or use Azure-provided DNS. You can choose to connect the network to on-premises or the Internet.

Internet Access and DNS

All resources can communicate with the Internet by default, via NAT. This can be restricted via NSGs and user routes. Inbound connectivity without SNAT requires a public IP. DNS in Azure can be Azure provided as a service by default, enabling resolution of everything within a VNet, or you can provide your own DNS server - a VM or virtual appliance deployed in Azure. For scenarios where only resolution within a VNet is required, use Azure DNS. For scenario where name resolution beyond a VNet, including on-prem resolution from VMs or resolution of Azure hostnames from on-prem systems - consider customer-managed DNS.

If you use custom DNS, VMs within a VNet must be restarted to take account of the change from default Azure managed DNS.

Network Security

Network Access Control, Firewalls, Securing remote access and cross-premises connectivity, Availability, Name Resolution. Global Traffic Routing, DDoS, Monitoring and Threat Detection, Logging & Audit.

Network Access Control - network layer controls - NSGs, Azure Security Center and Service Endpoints.

Resource control & forced tunneling - control routing behaviour on VNets with custom settings and shut down devices initiating connections on the Internet via Forced tunneling.

Virtual network security appliances enable a higher level of control beyond the network for greater protection.

Azure Firewall - cloud based firewalling to protect Azure network resources. A stateful firewall service for use when NSGs alone are not enough, and for compliance.

Secure remote connectivity - Individual workstations can be connected with point to site VPN, on-prem networks can be connected to VNets with a direct connect VPN or express route dedicated WAN link. VNets can also be connected to each other.

Availability can be improved via HTTP or network load balancing (Azure load balancer). Global load balancer traffic managers can be used for cross-region load balancing - Increase availability, increase performance.

Network Security Groups

An NSG is a traffic filter, allowing or restricting access to the network - they have inbound and outbound rules, and can be associated with a subnet or NIC. Rules defined by protocol, source and destination port, source and destination address, the direction, the priority and allow/deny. Rules are enforced based on priority, numbered 100 to 4096. The lower the number, the greater the priority.

NSG default tags can simplify rules - system provided groups of IP addresses - Virtual network, Azure Load Balancer, Internet.

Key networking limits

- 300 NICs (can increase to 1000)
- 100 NSGs (Can be 400)
- 200 NSG rules per NSG (can be 500)
- 100 user defined route tables (can be 400)
- 60 public IPs (can be raised by support call)
- 20 reserved IPs (can be raised by support call)

Azure Firewall

Built in HA. Supports availability zones - 99.95% available by default, 99.99% for multi-AZ. Can limit outbound HTTPS traffic or Azure SQL traffic to a specified list of FQDN including wildcards. Can centrally create allow or deny network filtering rules by source and destination IP address, port, and protocol. FQDN Tags for services can be used for rules, as can service tags for Microsoft managed services. Built in threat intelligence feed and both outbound SNAT and inbound DNAT support.

Azure Load Balancer

Basic/Standard load balancer - standard for balancing across VP IMs - public or private

Application gateway - Web application balancing, advanced features such as URL routing, also enables WAF

Traffic Manager - for global load balancing of applications and DNS management across regions

Basic load balancers are layer 4, support up to 100 instances, offer service monitoring, automated reconfiguration, hash-based distribution and both internal and public options.

Standard load balancers build on basic, but can support 1000 instances, any virtual machine in a single VNet with blended options supported - a mix of services. Supports HTPS. Supports availability zones and is secure by default.

While a basic load balancer is scoped to an availability set, the Standard Load Balancer is scoped to the entire VNet.

App Gateway is a Layer 7 application load balancer, enabling application level routing - cookie based session affinity, SSL offload and supports end-to-end SSL. WAF is also available with app gateway. URL-based content routing available. Requires its own subnet, and is highly available supporting multi-az.

App gateways available in 2-page response configs and 4 sizes: 6K/100K page responses - small is 7.5/35Mbps, Medium is 13/100Mbps and Large is 50/200Mbps.

Traffic manager is DNS-level load balancing for Internet -facing applications. Monitoring supported via HTTP/HTTPS GET - Azure VMs, Cloud services, web apps and external endpoints.

Hybrid connectivity options

Site to Site VPN
ExpressRoute - dedicated WAN link
Point to site VPN

S2S requires a VPN gateway with a public IP, and VPN established to a datacentre VPN device also with a public IP. Multiple sites can be connected. No overlapping addresses to avoid routing problems. S2S VPN connections over IPsec/IKEv1 or v2 VPN tunnel. Requires a publicly routable IP on both ends, and the customer location cannot be behind NAT. S2S connections can be used for cross-premises and hybrid configurations.

Point to site is a number of individual devices VPNing in to Azure via VPN gateway - possibly via jump box or Citrix. No need for a VPN device or public IP, just an Internet connection - supported by Windows 7, 8, 8.1 and 10 as well as all server revisions from 2008 R2. Throughput can be up to 100Mbps, albeit unreliable owing to the Internet. Does not scale well though, so only useful for small numbers of users.

VPN Gateway SKUs

Basic - 10 VNet to VNet tunnels, 128 P2S connections, 100 Mbps aggregate throughput benchmark.

VpnGw1 - 30 VNet to VNet tunnels, 128 P2S connections, 650 Mbps aggregate throughput benchmark.

VpnGw2 - 30 VNet to VNet tunnels, 128 P2S connections, 1 Gbps aggregate throughput benchmark.

VpnGw3 - 30 VNet to VNet tunnels, 128 P2S connections, 1.2 Gbps aggregate throughput benchmark.

Recommended Gw1,2 or 3 for production use.
ExpressRoute is a dedicated circuit between customer and Azure. Enables connectivity to private and public services over the dedicated link. Connectivity models include cloud exchange co-location, dedicated point to point or any to any IPVPN connection over mpls WAN network. ExpressRoute provides Layer 3 connectivity between customer and Azure. Connectivity to all regions within a

geopolitical region, and a premium add-on is available for truly global connectivity. Dynamic BGP routing and redundancy with each peering location is available.

You need an Azure subscription, a relationship with a carrier and the physical work complete to enable the ExpressRoute connectivity. Then you can make the order, including choosing the peering location, bandwidth, billing model and standard/premium. You are then provided with a service key, which is passed to the connectivity provider, VPN IDs are also provided. Connectivity then established and peering can be set up.

/30 subnets required for peering setup - one for path 1, another for path 2. VLAN ID for peering, ASN for Perring, ExpressRoute ASN=12076, and an optional MD5 hash are required for private and public peering. Microsoft peering also requires advertised prefixes (public IP), customer ASN, RIR/IRR for IP and ASN validation.

Unlimited vs Metered billing. Both offer speeds from 50Mbps to 10Gps, unlimited inbound data. Outbound data is unlimited in the Unlimited tier but charged per GB in the metered tier. That unlimited outbound comes at a higher monthly fee.

Routing and Peering

Every subnet has a route for the Local Vnet, On-premises (Vnet Gateway next hop) and the Internet (Internet gateway next hop). Default routing - for anything within the VNet, route to local VNet. If the address is within the on-prem address prefixes or BGP published routes, route to Gateway.

If the address is not within the VPN or on-prem, route to the Internet via NAT. If the destination is an Azure DC address and ER public peering is available, route to gateway. If the destination is an Azure DC with S2S or an ER without public peering enabled, route to Host NAT for Internet path, but it never leaves the datacenter. User defined routes can be created as required.

VNet peering can enable VNets to communicate with each other - only works point to point / hub and spoke - not possible to transient peer - like AWS.

ExpressRoute is the better option for privacy and security (no Internet) and bandwidth, since you are not reliant on the transient nature of Internet conditions. A hybrid connection can be used to allow a web app to talk to the on-prem datacenter. The hybrid connection manager can be installed on Server 2008 with .net framework 4.5+ and windows management framework 4.0+. Windows Server

2012 with Windows framework 4.0+, or Windows Server 2012 R2.

Azure Monitoring

Monitor and Visualise metrics, query and analyse logs, setup, and alert actions. Host level metrics are collected by default. If you want guest level as well, select a storage account and update diagnostic settings.

Log Analytics performs the central role with everything filtered into it. Data sources are connected to (VMs, Apps, services, and resources) and other log analytics sources such as security center and app insights can be piped here too. Search queries are available to output the data as required. Log analytics receives log data from multiple sources, indexes and sorts it into tables automatically and makes it available for consumption in a variety of ways.

Data Sources include:

Custom Log - <LogName>_CL - text files on Windows or Linux agents containing log data.

Windows Event Logs - Event - Events collected from event:logon on Windows machines.

Windows Performance Counters - Perf - Performance counters from Windows machines.

Linux Performance Counters - Perf - Performance counters from Linux machines.

IIS Logs - W3CIISLog - IIS Logs in W3C format.

Syslog - Syslog events on Windows or Linux machines.

Search query fundamentals - start with source table, follow on with operators, separating additional operations by using pipes. Use the 'union' command to join other tables and workspaces to a query. Resource names in queries are case sensitive.

Backup

High Availability - Availability sets are essentially multiple instances on standby to take the load should one fail.

Disaster Recovery - run apps in a second datacenter for recovery in the event of failure. Backup - Restore data in the event of system failure.

Azure Backup is a cloud backup solution, unlimited scale, and data transfer. Multiple storage options - LRS & GRS - GRS is default which makes sense - spread data across geolocations to avoid losing it all. LRS is three copies within a zone. Long term retention - you can keep data as long as you like, up to a maximum of 9999 recovery points. Application consistent backups, depending on the application. And Data encryption is available.

Components - Azure Backup agent (MARS) allows for file level restore, system state restore. Systems center DPM (data protection manager), Azure Backup Server and Azure IaaS VM Backup. Snapshot recovery is also available and uses underlying Blob storage to take snapshots of VM page blobs - can be copied to the same or different regions.

The VM can then be rebuilt from the snapshot. The backup is application-consistent, but only if shutdown gracefully when the snapshot was taken. Otherwise it is crash-consistent. Geo-replication is another recovery option, using

Azure storage GRS - data is replicated to a paired region far awa from the primary, to make it recoverable in the event of an outage or region failure. RA-GRS option also available.

Azure Site Recovery (ASR)

Disaster Recovery for running apps in a second DC to cover failure events. On-prem to Azure recovery tool - VMWare and Hyper-V to Azure replication, Azure to Azure recovery - recover workloads from your primary region in a secondary target region, Automation and Orchestration - set up recovery plans to customise the order in which services are restored, as well as any subsequent scripts that need to be run. Integrate into Azure Automation for additional requirements. RTO and RPO targets - continuous replication for Azure, VMWare, and Hyper-V.

ASR replication frequency - 30 seconds, 5 minutes, or 15 minutes.

A VMWare to Azure migration comes in 3 phases – Convert VM to a VHD, Upload to Azure and the Migration completes from the recovery vault.

Prepare Azure: Verify account permissions to create a VM in the resource group and selected network, and write to the storage account), prepare VMWare, and stop recovery. Create a storage account, create recovery services vault, setup an Azure network. Prepare VMWare: VMWare permissions, prepare account for mobility service installation, verify compatibility, and prepare connectivity to Azure VMs.

Recovery Options

VMs available in the event of region outage = Azure Site Recovery, and GRS storage
Individual recovery of data for specific service - Azure backup, 3rd party backup technologies
Highly available application across regions - traffic manager, load balancers in each region, availability sets/zones in each region

Good Luck!

The Exam when I took it had just been released, and featured 55 questions – mostly multiple choice with a few drag and drop 'put the required operations in the right order' type questions and finally a couple of cases studies. The case studies provide lots of supporting information is around a fictional company – their users, groups, networks, resources, requirements and so on – and then ask questions based on that information.

It was a 3hr exam, it took me around an hour. My head hurt by the end, and I found it a challenge... but I hope you win as I did! You will also find the material for AZ-303 is very similar!

This book, plus the information I gathered studying AZ-900, and a decent familiarity with the Azure Portal, were all I needed to pass AZ-104 and become a Microsoft Azure Certified Administrator!

Contacting the Author

If you have any comments on this book, questions for me or suggestions for the next edition you can contact me at the following address:

publications@blackchili.co.uk.

You will find my professional profile on LinkedIn here:

https://www.linkedin.com/in/renhimself/

Printed in Great Britain
by Amazon

37771217R00037